A PORTRAIT OF A BROKEN HEART

LOVE IN THE FORM OF POETRY; OF TODAY ,TOMORROW AND YESTERDAY .

DAVID T NICHOLAS

This book is dedicated to every girl ,woman whom i have loved
over the years and still love

To those of whom have broken my heart .

To every girl and woman i came across in my life where we
sparked love let it be in a small way or big this is for you .

To anyone who has been "A potrait of a brokenheart" this one is
specially for you because i understand what you have gone thru .

Contents

Contents

1. The theory of sight in love

Love, is such a strange little thing
It goes to great heights with out wings
And even goes deep down without fins.
The stranger thing about love is
You can still feel without touching
You can see with your eyes closed
You can talk without talking
The Concealment of love we never know
The sight becomes blinded
Almost everything seems suffice
As long as both are in a hanker
All will seem upside when one begins to incline
In the simplest words to say ;
Everything in love seems fair
But once kaput
Everything just seems unfair.

2. Two painful Love Stories can never be the same.

This love I bore
Not to weep and sore
But to last a lifetime and bring forth
my offspring and future generation
But instead a one so loved
Has been lost and gone
And a feeling in me
As if the living life
Is as lifeless as can be
No words to describe the
Love story that God has written for me
For I do not deserve this
Nor does any helpless or love lost do
For I so loved a girl
And can pledge with all my heart
That I truly did
I doubt the same back from her
She very well dupled in love
What's strange is all in a short span
She managed to treble love

And marry the third

If this is the way my love story to be said

Of how I Morn and bleed

Let this not be written in anyone's life again

For two painful Love Stories

can never be the same .

3. A feeling like forever and never

It's really feels good
To fall in love all over again
But the thought of not being accepted
Or that your heart might be broken again
Makes you really think if it's really love
But love comes in ways we don't know
It's come in a strange Little way back to me
If it is what it is then my life has a
Chance to be loved again
A love so silent and dwelling
So secret and strong within
A feeling like forever and never
The very way how true love is felt.

4. Love at a funeral

I met a girl at her grandmother's funeral
It was love at first sight I must tell.
She was so pretty that I fell
She felt the same about me I could tell.
Her name Starts with S
I wouldn't tell you but would like you to guess
I couldn't believe it was all happening
All the talking with our eyes
I was really shy but had to be wise
She spoke and broke the spell away
The beauty in her eyes just swept me away
The story carried on I must say
Till today I love her the same way
But now that she's gotten away
For her to come back in my heart I pray
In a very special way
How we met in a very strange little way .

5. What do Lover's do

What do Lover's do
when the sun is very bright
on a sunny summer's set

What do Lover's do
when the wind is biting cold
on a windy winters week

What do Lover's do
when the trees shed their leaves
on a shedding springs season

What do Lover's do
when the trees bear new leaves and fruits
on an alluring autumns age

What do Lover's do
when the clouds are dark and heavy falls
with a runny rolling rain

What do Lover's do
when the moon and stars shine
in the nightly night's nest

I guess they do the same
on a sunny summer,windy winter,
shedding spring, alluring autumn, rolling rain,
and in the nightly night's nest
they just make love
and keep on loving each other
changing according to the seasons
with love and everlasting life.

6. My dear C

My dear C
What have I ever done
Before meeting you
For after which a feeling that
Has no word to be expressed
Has taken over me .
A feeling of love filled with hurt and sorrow
Does the word Saudade suite me
I can't really tell
For every minute that passes by
The hate and love I have for you just grows

7. My first kiss

It is a feeling
That a lifetime can't give
A moment captured
And that can never
Be erased or forgotten
Thou the memory
Is a special and unforgettable,
Or something that can't be erased
We remember every pixel of the moment
But what's really hard to tell is
While kissing did the upper lip
Touch first or did the lower
Keep thinking about it
And you will definitely want to
Try and do it again
And want the first kiss
You got be the kiss of a lifetime.

8. kiss on a photograph

Most photographs capture moments
That we all want to treasure
And in due course when we Come Across
That photograph that is really dear to us
We have some time or the other
kissed some photograph
especially which means the world to us
but kissing the one when we are in love
when we are young is a heavenly feeling
And it is worse when you get caught
Because your lip marks remain on the photograph
and it is in the hands of the one you love
What happens next and what moments we share
Will always remain memories close to our hearts.

9. The memories we created

All the memories
That we have created together
Are the only ones I look upon
And wish they would come back again
And I could relive every moment again
Or we both Live together forever
Creating and recreation of memories
Don't you ever stop or take the time
To think or remember all the memories
That we both had together
For if you ever Do
The memories That we created
Would keep us together for life
And never ever make us apart.

10. love is like the moon

Love is like the moon
It keeps changing every day
But it will remain
And be called the same
it will come and go
But never vanish completely
those that embrace it
during its changing phases
shall be rewarded when
it is fully bright and illuminated

11. By your side

What if the one you love
Closes their eyes
Right when by your side
And never awakes
Long after they are gone
Will the love you had
For them Fadeaway
Or take you into
A trans of blues
Thinking about the thoughts
That by your side
She held your hand
That by your side
She hugged you and slept
That By your side
she never did wake up again.

12. The minute I met you

The second I met you
You were inevitable.
I wanted to do all the
Things lovers do in splits of a second
Then the second you held my finger
The slightest touch gave me
A feeling of mixed
Emotions and thoughts Called love
Every heartbeat something
Was magically happening
And It all happened
The minute I met you

13. My love was like

My love was like
The burning sun
The darkest night
The biting bitter cold
The colourless sky
Threatening clouds
The angry windy winds
The drowning rains
The furious storm
The Earth-shaking thunder
The stikes of lightning
The frozen cold ice
The billowing fog
All put together was what
My heart, mind, body and soul
Was what my love was like.
The feelings are strange;
But I was in love, still am in
love with the person
who gave me these
And left me alone to love myself
which will never happen.

14. A potrait of a broken heart

Just because I was so strong
I never showed my feelings,
Never had anyone to share them with,
I would portray an outer image of myself
To the world and onlookers
A portrait of a broken heart
Of which I painted on the outside
With brightness, smiles, happiness, laughter
Lovingness and no regret image
But the inside of the portrait
A dark black sadness,
Of pixels so black and dark
that could never be mixed
with any colour to make it bright
The portrait of a broken heart
It can never be understood
Unless you really care or love
The portrait-like yourself
So much has it gone thru
For you to see the final image
And to hide the first strokes
Of what it has gone thru.

One can never really understand
The Portrait of a broken heart.

15. Mentally despair in love

I could never hurt you physically
Nor could I hurt you mentally
I even couldn't hurt myself physically
Neither could I Stop myself
From getting being mentally despair
The thoughts of you not being with me
Have already taken a troll over me
And the thought of not seeing you again
The thought of me not spending
The rest of my life with you
Had taken me into depths
Of wretchedness and drowned
Me so deep that one would be
Lost trying to find a surface to breathe again
I couldn't portray it to anyone
But just showed a calm outer appearance.

16. Love can never be erased

Love is never like
Writing with a pencil
On a piece of paper
But writing on a piece
Of paper with a pen
The ink we write
It remains like a permanent mark
It can never be erased.
Once stained by love or ink
It can never be erased
If tried will remain
Like a stain forever
Just destruction is
The only measure of erasing
The ink from the paper
So is death that can
Put an end to you
Heartbroken blue miserable life.

17. Neither Heaven Nor Hell

You showed me what heaven
Looks like.
And what hell
Looks like too.
I want neither of the two
Because in it we never
Lasted forever.
I want something or someplace
No matter what happens
We both are there always
Together forever.

18. Love (Cinquain)

Love

Me, you

Both us, together

Mixed emotions and feelings

Love

19. What really kills in love

I never care how difficult
Being together will be
I could make it right
Make a lot of sacrifices
Just to be by your side.
but really is a scare for me
Is not being together.
Because I know once
We are apart
There's nothing in
A lifetime I could do
To bring you back to me
There is nothing worse
Then being apart from you.
What kills more is seeing you
Or even the thought of you
With someone else are like
A million needles constantly
Pricking my heart and my mind.

20. I was your pastime

I was your pastime
These are the words you told me.
It broke my heart when you said so
You told me that you were
Just using me
because you had no one else
And I was jobless
since I had a lot of time
To love you and do whatever
You told me to do.
Till you got used to the new city
New lifestyle, new people
And was ok to live on you're own
In the city
I was just your pastime
And will be your pastime'
Towards the end
That's what you done
You shattered my heart
Into a million pieces
That can never be fixed even
If you loved me back a million times
I thought you would come back

And love me once again
But you came back
To break my heart into
A million pieces more
This time in an unforgivable way.

21. When in love

when in love everything
will seem meaningful
when not in love everything
will seem meaningless
In love, everything will be synonymous
when not everything will be anonymous
And if faith in love is lost
The world that was beautiful loses its beauty.
Songs will lose their charm,
Flowers lose their fragrance,
Words lose their meaning and become meaningless
Most of all your life
And the life of the ones around you
Becomes sad disheartened and joyless
Everything is never the same
When in love.

22. I wish love was ...

I wish Love
Was without borders
At times we do get
The feeling that it doesn't
But we mostly have a border
To choose from when in love.
Of whether we can fall in love,
With whom we can love
And whom we mustn't.
Your choice of love
Has already been decided
Unless and until
You cross all odds and boundaries
I wish I could love one
And so many the same.
love always comes with borders
I wish it just doesn't .

23. Walking alone

There's a lot of difference
When we are walking alone
And walking
With someone by our side.
Especially walking
With the one we love
Every step that we take
Is carefully watched over.
Ensuring the walk we have
Is a safe and guided walk.
A feeling or something
We would never Experience
Walking Alone.

When we see everyone
Walking with someone,
And we are walking alone
It saddens your heart.
What's worse is when you lose
The one you truly love
And have to take
The walk of life all alone.
Then you realize the real difference

And the real pain of walking
With somebody by your side
And walking alone.

24. Time to meet the one you love

when the time to meet
The one you love
Every second you wait
Feels like an hour.
The time you are
with the one you love
every hour you spend
Feels like a second
when it passes by.
while waiting for the one you love
The thoughts of what you are to do
with the one you love
The second you meet them
Runs Crazily in your head
keeps running constantly in you
It is something that cant be expressed
But can be demonstrated
when you meet the one you love
Not all words and thoughts are said and done
But it is full of surprises and love
I've had my share of it
if you have waited

when the time to meet
The one you love came
you will agree
It is insanely beautiful.

25. Death do not us apart

I got this crazly little feeling
That you're really special to me
I just wanna spend my life with you
No matter what we both go thru
Now and forever,
Till the end.
May even death do us not apart
I'll always be with you.
Love you till the end of times
Love you till the moon
Comes out in the noon
And the sun
Comes out in the night sky.
When in love
The only thing we truly wish
That may even
Death do us not apart.

26. BrokenHearted (Cinquain)

Brokenhearted
The Saddest,
love becomes two
together then, separated now
Brokenhearted.

27. Nothing is gonna bring you back

Nothing's gonna bring you back
I guess you're just dead to me
Because you have a heart of stone
I've tried so hard to get you back
Into my life but it made no difference
Because you never cared
Or moved an inch towards my love
All I know is that you gone
And I could try or do all I want
I can pray for you to come back
Or fight against the world
But Nothing is gonna bring you back .

28. Always love man

Always love man for when
man is in love it's love that he spreads
If man is being hated
It's hatred that he spreads.
A man without love is a monster
And a monster with love is a man.
After all, that man goes thru in life
It's a little love that he longs for
If he doesn't get it
He finds it in many different ways
Because he knows life is all about love
It's the most beautiful and
needed aspect in our life
Love, for love alone, can love you back.

29. Bad choice

Have I made a bad choice
By choosing you in the crowd
Over another who could have
Been my world for the rest of my life.
I guess this is how life is
Sometimes bad choices we make
Later on in life, we regret.
But falling in love with you
Was the best choice
And perhaps one
Of the bad choices
I have made in my life'
Life brings you closer
To the people
Who would love you now
And hate you later
Hate you now
And love you later.
Ask yourself if it
Really a bad choice
Or the way of life.

30. How young is young To fall in love?

How young is young
To fall in love?
Especially the days
Of the millennials
Love has lost it's really meaning
In the modern and digital world
Everyone is using the words
I love you in many ways
and the most being in a lustful way
Which doesn't do any justice to love
The real connection between the two is lost
Nothing truly felt
Nothing truly lost
Nothing truly gained
Is not what is love all about
It's a special connection you feel
Towards someone no matter
Who, how or what they are.
but ask yourself this question
How young is young
To fall in love?
Because everyone you fall

In love these days

Are already in love

Or have deeply been in love.

• 37 •

31. If Love is all that you desire

If love is all you desire
You find yourself in a mire
And if love for you is the only cure
You will definitely try to endure
So that you find the love your hearts desire.
Love is a feeling that arises
From deep within
It can come in any form
It can be towards anyone at any time.
If Love is all that you desire
You will have your fair chance of love
Might be for a minute
Might be for a day
Might be for a week
Might be for a month
Might be for a year
love will come in the unexpected hour
If love is all that you desire
so be ready to accept it when it arrives.

32. An ode to love

Love is never you
Love is always two.
Love is always love
But each time it's anew
Of which We can't construe.
Loving you was all I thought
Of when I was with you and not
Ever since my eyes laid eyes on you
Love was the only thing
I could think of.
An ode to love
Is an ode to you
Words to embrace you
I would say
Each time in a different way
But all in all, meant the same
I love you
Love is not me or you
Love is both together
That is us,
An ode to love.

• 40 •

33. The colour of love

The colour of love
Is red.
May be another for some.
it doesn't really matter
When in love it's all beautiful
But when broken
It changes to black
Everything which once was bright
Becomes dark all of a sudden.
When the colour of love changes
It changes all the colours around us
Especially the colours of life
You're loved one changes
Their colour first
The shades of colours
Around you change,
People around change,
You're thoughts become darker
And deeper from what
You always thought about life
Be careful in life
For the colour of love
Will definitely change

And when they change
It can change
The colour of your life.

• 42 •

By

David T Nicholas

34. A forgotten lad

I was in love
I always wanted to be,
To be in someone's heart
And be held in one's arms
Be in their mind and never begotten
Life takes another turn
For me and nothing did I learn
Pain, grief and suffering I earn
No one's heart, no one's arms
In no one's mind
Perhaps never loved at all
Or even if falsely did get loved
Each and every time I fall in love
I'm just another forgotten lad.

35. Moments in love

The feeling of love can be
Compared with that of apricity
In love, we mostly brable
And often feel our loves grubble
When together we are grufeling
Anything other than love or the
One so near and dear to our heart
All just seem trumpery-
We love them though they are churlish
Accept the fact of a philodox
We often see each other.
A lot of things we do for love
A lot of things we bear
With a lot of mixed emotions
And feelings we care.

36. A maladroit in love

My love is like a baritone
That is; lower than tenor
And is higher than brass
Whose feelings are smudged by both
And never truly know
Not waiting for a capstone
And can be compared to a sousaphone
And made to be an undertone
While that of another a methadone
I feel so dejected
A life of solitary lone
I fell in love I was adroit
But in the end, I'm left maladroit.

37. Life's deplorable

If love is the only best thing
In this world of ours
Then it's obviously even the worst.
Would I bury the broken love I had
Yes, I would and I wouldn't
For a love so true, would have.
Thought of both abdication
Of my feelings deep inside
I wish someone, be an imitator
Of my life to see
What I've gone through
But it isn't the way
Life is, it's mostly I must
Say deplorable.

38. Whatever's in that mind of yours

Whatever's in that mind of yours
Nobody just knows
Whether it's love
Or whether it's hate
Could be anything too
for you just anyone thing
They would do.
They'll keep growing too
And try to define who you are
Or maybe you'll judge
The world as seen by you
Most might not be true
Now whatever's in that mind of yours
Nobody just knows.

39. My greatest fear

My greatest fear is
The closer I get to you
And then one day
When you are far apart from me
The fear of drowning myself
In life's deepest sorrows and
Lifelessness is certain
When the certainty
Of my life is certain
Can give life a chance to drown
As failure and sorrowfulness
Are nothing new to me
They come and go
As often as night and day.
But cease to go away like
The night and day do.

40. Will I ever find someone

If I ever love someone
Will they love me back the same
Or if they don't love me as I do
Do I solely have myself to blame
Even after telling the world their name
Will, i ever find someone
Who would love me just the same
Just the way I love them
And shout to the world
Feeling proud
With my name alongside theirs.
Will, i ever find someone,
Tell me will I ever find someone.